How to Score Your First or Next Million-Dollar Gift

By Jim Eskin

Founder of Eskin Fundraising Training, LLC

ISBN 979-8-218-49426-1

Printed by Litho Press, Inc., San Antonio, Texas

 ESKIN
FUNDRAISING
TRAINING

Visit the website at www.eskinfundraisingtraining.com
or send email to the author at jeskin@aol.com.

How to Score Your First or Next Million-Dollar Gift

Dr. Lance Brouthers

Dedication

One of the wake-up calls to getting older is when you lose friends not of your parent's generation, but contemporaries. It's painful to realize that you will never see or speak to them again. I've begun to lose such friends, and to be frank, I didn't quite anticipate the impact. It made me realize that you can make new friends, but you will never have the chance to make old friends, with whom you shared significant chunks of your life. One such friend was Dr. Lance Brouthers, a brilliant scholar and educator who partnered with me in developing the proposal for my first million-dollar gift. His primary research interest was international business strategy and emerging markets and their global implications. Lance was a prolific researcher and author of scholarly publications. He provided leadership at several institutions of higher learning where he was instrumental in nurturing doctoral programs, including The University of Texas at San Antonio (UTSA), where our paths crossed. As much as his intellectual achievements distinguished him, he was also a good guy with broad and surprising interests including an amazing collection of comics and other memorabilia of Superman and other action heroes. A heavy man, he loved food, and we shared a mutual interest in outstanding deli food. After he left San Antonio, we enjoyed weekly hour-long phone conversations, poking fun at our political differences, but always concluding on a high note with spirited discussions of our favorite hometown sports teams — his from Cleveland, mine from Boston. He passed away in September 2022, close to the time I lost my close high school friend, Dr. Jon Mark. Their losses reinforced my commitment not to pass up any opportunities to stay connected to those individuals from the past who gave me the most precious gift of all — friendship.

Contents

Foreword

The Council for Resource Development (CRD) that served as a clearinghouse for the professional development and networking of advancement staff among community colleges, brought Jim Eskin and I together. The highlight of the CRD calendar annually was a national conference in Washington, D.C. every Fall. As fortune would have it back in 2010, Jim attended one of my presentations, and the following year, I had the opportunity to participate in one of his.

It was immediately apparent that he loved what he was doing presenting to colleagues on all aspects of the donor cycle, and especially personal major gift solicitations. Keep in mind that most CRD members at that time, while very good at their jobs, were much more familiar with corporate relations and grantsmanship (especially government grants) than private philanthropy. Our work to open their eyes to the noteworthy potential of deeper alumni and friend relationships and growing far more robust major gifts programs within annual fund and campaign endeavors, drew us even closer.

Before heading back home after that 2011 conference, we huddled together and discovered a mutual passion for capacity building and life-long learning and life-long sharing. This conversation led to our plans to organize a planning retreat for Jim's board at Alamo Colleges Foundation. We worked diligently over the next couple of months to craft an agenda focusing on many proven ways board members can contribute to fundraising success, even without ever asking for a gift themselves.

As can happen, despite our planning and best intentions, the board decided to engage in a free-wheeling discussion of many other topics — curriculum, government relations, public relations, and others — but kept away from our fundraising focus. Jim and I had to immediately go to Plan B: Just let the board members talk about issues that were on their minds. They loved doing so and considered the retreat an unqualified success.

As Jim and I debriefed after the experience, our bond and appreciation for each other's instincts, skills and personalities deepened. In many ways we were kindred spirits obsessed with the art and science of fundraising, making it more friendly to those whose inclination was to fear it.

In fact, these early experiences together were formative in nature as the Institute for

Philanthropic Excellence went from an idea to an emerging national consulting firm dedicated to serving smaller, fledgling organizations across the non-profit spectrum. Together, with our team of 40 professionals based all around the country, we have assisted in the enhancement and expansion of philanthropic programs for more than 100 organizations coast-to-coast, helping them to understand that even the "little guys" can enjoy greater levels of success by turning the fundraising pyramid on its point.

I have to admit that, for the next several years, as Jim and I contemplated many campaign scenarios for Alamo Colleges Foundation, where Jim served as Executive Director for nine years, we never convinced his board to move things forward. While I didn't sign on a new client partner, I ended up with a reward much richer and satisfying … a friend for life, and a comrade in arms.

Since launching Eskin Fundraising Training in 2018, he has sponsored more than 250 live workshops and/or webinars focusing on a target audience of smaller non-profits. I am proud to claim that I've enjoyed helping co-present and participate in more of these programs than anyone else.

It is no exaggeration to declare that Jim is fanatical about his commitment to being innovative, creative, and most importantly, both informative and enjoyable in his wide variety of educational programs to empower non-profits to more effectively embrace the principles, strategies and best practices that culminate in stronger gift income results.

The topic of this book is deeply personal to me. There are so many deserving non-profits that will benefit from the contents. I fully appreciate the sentiment for those who have not attained a million-dollar gift yet that it may appear at first like an unreachable star. It isn't! My team and I have been there for numerous such celebrations.

How wonderful that Jim has, yet again, blessed us all with an entirely readable and highly informative guide to elevate success and impact.

Marvin R. LeRoy, Jr.
President & Founder
Institute for Philanthropic Excellence

Magic Moments:
First Million Dollar Gifts

Friday, December 4th, 1998, seems like yesterday to me. At 11:15 a.m. I was in the Dean's Office in the College of Business at The University of Texas at San Antonio (UTSA). For the first time in my career, I had just asked for a million-dollar gift … and the response was YES! I wanted to shout for joy but restrained myself as my boss just tactfully blinked at me.

The donor was an odd choice to become the first million-dollar donor in UTSA history. Richard S. Liu, Founder of Superior Leather, in Hong Kong, 8,269 miles away from San Antonio. But his gift to UTSA made perfect sense. In 1974, Dr. Jim Gaertner, who would later become Dean of UTSA's College of Business (and my boss), was Controller of Tandy Brands in Yoakum, Texas. That was the year that Richard made his first trip to the U.S. and his first big sale to Tandy Brands — a sale that he never forgot. Jim and Richard developed a friendship that grew closer as their career paths progressed. As Richard's company became one of the leading leather manufacturers in the world, he began to become a generous philanthropist making gifts to prestigious institutions such as the University of California-Berkeley.

One day in the summer of 1998, Jim stepped into my office and for the first-time mentioned Richard and his exciting gift capacity and demonstrated philanthropy. We decided to craft a million-dollar proposal to fund student and faculty exchanges between UTSA and prominent universities in China. Richard scheduled a trip to San Antonio. At that point, I didn't know what to expect. While he had been generous to other institutions, he had never given a penny to us. But now, we were going to ask him for more than just pennies. I had watched Jim on dozens of occasions ask for much more modest amounts, but this time he was inviting me to do the ask. His reasoning was that a successful seven-digit solicitation would do more for my career than for his. He was absolutely right. After his first million-dollar gift, Richard subsequently made gifts of $5 million more to UTSA.

My next million-dollar solicitation could not have been to someone more different. Dr. Janice Mendelson, a distinguished retired Army colonel and surgeon, had been making modest gifts to my next employer, Our Lady of the Lake University, a small Catholic institution in San Antonio. Almost everyone thought she was just eccentric. Characteristically, she would always come to meetings with miscellaneous paperwork stuffed in plastic supermarket bags. She lived an incredibly modest life in the same small apartment for 20 years and drove an older model Toyota Corolla. Her passion was for folk dance and its capacity to bring people of diverse backgrounds closer together. In fact, during her service in the Vietnam War she organized folk dances.

Janice didn't believe in calendared meetings keeping to a strict schedule. Discussions with her just wandered aimlessly. Everyone reminded me that this was Janice just being Janice, and I should not take her seriously. Unfortunately, I believed them – until one of my friends and colleagues, Gloria Urrabazo, met with Janice after I did. Gloria cautioned me against jumping to conclusions, insisting that Janice deserved closer attention. I realized it was necessary to meet Janice in unrushed settings, such as early Saturday evening dinners at her favorite diner. (It helped that she took a strong liking to my wife Andrea.)

Slowly but surely, I earned her trust, and a major gift became a possibility. We realized that serious discussions needed to be conducted with her attorneys but without Janice present. We hammered out a multi-part $2.2 million gift agreement in 2005 composed of three components: current dollars to fund a folk center program, an endowment to continue support of the folk center program in perpetuity, plus a $500,000 unrestricted gift (which would be primarily used to establish athletic programs that played a huge role in reviving enrollment). Unlike my role in asking for the gift from Richard Liu, this time I had the opportunity to play the primary cultivation role in building the friendship and securing the gift from Dr. Mendelson.

When I became Executive Director of Alamo Colleges Foundation in 2009, the potential of a major gift from Kerrville businessman Neil Griffith had been lingering for too long. He grew up poor as one of 10 children in Arkansas and was able to attend college on the G.I. Bill. This changed the direction of his life, and he never forgot it. In getting to know him better, I also learned Mr. Griffith couldn't stand waste. I vividly recall that, one day as I was walking with him to his car, he expressed the need to return to the office to pick up a yellow pad, which turned out to have just one sheet of paper left on it. Knowing his characteristic of being thrifty would be valuable as I moved forward in making the ask.

But talks progressed at a snail's pace. Mr. Griffith was very interested in funding an endowed scholarship for a new satellite campus in Kerrville, about 60 miles west of San Antonio. I was never scared of writing assignments and bringing them to fruition to the satisfaction of all those involved. So I decided to pack up my laptop and hold a series of face-to-face meetings with Mr. Griffith's designated representative, John Spikes. Section by section we discussed the contents of a five-page gift agreement. At the end of each session, Spikes would review our progress with Mr. Griffith.

In 2010 we came to an agreement on a $1 million endowed scholarship, and I finally had the opportunity to meet Mr. Griffith at the opening of the Kerrville Center. As is sometimes the case, we encountered difficulty finding enough students to apply for and receive a scholarship. To move forward, I was able to begin a personal relationship with Mr. Griffith as we discussed possibilities to loosen restrictions on scholarship criteria. He informed me that he was going to give us another $2.5 million and wanted discussions on how best to allocate and spend the money. His first request was to add another $1 million to the endowed scholarship fund, keep in mind that we were experiencing challenges in awarding just $1 million. So we then held several face-to-face meetings to discuss possibilities on the best use of the remaining $1.5 million.

The Kerrville area is home to major hospitals with a strong demand for health care professionals, especially nurses, so he agreed to commit $750,000 to construction of new facilities for nursing programs. Recognizing the huge value of flexible unrestricted funds, we were able to convince him to commit the other $500,000 to an endowed fund to be spent each year at the discretion of the Kerrville Center Director. In February 2017 we announced this $2.4 million gift — a new record for Alamo Colleges Foundation.

Fundraisers, particularly in the area of leadership gifts, achieve the greatest impact not by the gifts they solicit themselves, but how they leverage the relationships and abilities of others on their professional teams and boards. A terrific example is my experience with a $1 million gift Alamo Colleges Foundation received from the indomitable Harvey E. Najim, one of the most energetic forces for doing good I've ever had the pleasure of meeting. At the heart of his philanthropic personality is a genuine affinity for the underdog. He enjoys connecting with people from all walks of life, particularly those who directly benefit from his gifts. He understands and respects them. He has a laser-like focus on children's needs, especially for food, shelter, clothing, and medical treatment. He has a passion for the promise of education.

Harvey is a classic self-made American success story. Discovering the power of computers, he went on to build Sirius Computer Solutions into a $1.7 billion corporation. His philanthropic jumping-off moment came in 2006 after a Private Equity Transaction, when he launched the Harvey E. Najim Family Foundation (now named Najim Charitable Foundation). He's enjoyed giving away money more than making it. It's challenging to keep up with his philanthropy which, between personal and foundation giving, is approximately $200 million, and he is making plans for that total to reach $250 million.

My major gifts officer, Deborah Martin, the best hire I ever made, played the pivotal role in working closely with Harvey culminating in 2016 with a $2 million gift (including generous portions for four-year institutions) establishing the Harvey Najim Pathways Scholarship. This empowered some 200 low-income students (50 per year over four years) to begin their higher education journey at a local community college then transfer to local public universities to earn baccalaureate degrees and earn jobs in Information Technology, Cyber-Security, Nursing and Health Professions. The return on this philanthropic investment is exciting careers for San Antonio students and estimated at contributing $10 million to $12 million each year to the local economy. This innovative initiative was very much of Harvey's hands-on design. Deborah was the primary resource in furnishing Harvey with much-needed research and data to design and implement a successful program.

Harvey and I nurtured our friendship through this partnership. Since then, Harvey emerged as a cherished mentor and reservoir of support as I pivoted from practitioner to fundraising trainer/consultant. In fact, he was the first person I met with when developing plans for this career transition. He generously shared his time to speak in five live gatherings and/or webinars, some attracting overflow audiences of more than 150 non-profit leaders. I would not have attained my position in the fundraising world without the visibility and rich guidance he provided.

In his latest chapter he continues serve as chairman of the board but has turned over the day-to-day leadership of the foundation to his long-time executive director and chief operating officer so he can devote more time to mentoring students in the Najim Center for Business Innovation and Career Advancement at UTSA. He is also writing a book to share the insights gained from having built from scratch a leading technology company, and the many lessons he's learned from being a change agent in the philanthropic world.

It needs to be emphasized how vastly different the personalities of these four donors were who made record-setting gifts to each of my employers. Their backgrounds, motivations and philanthropic visions were different. They required different strategies and approaches to arrive at consensus. The common denominator was meeting the donors where they were, listening closely, always keeping an eye out for clues, and being sufficiently patient and providing the time to make crucial decisions. Donors are unique and require their own cultivation, solicitation and stewardship techniques.

My Journey

I'm not bragging, but I have a dream job. I'm happy doing precisely what I want to do. I can apply every skill, experience and lesson I have been fortunate enough to learn over the course of my career to a wholly satisfying endeavor. Without a doubt, this is the most rewarding phase of my career and my life.

Why? Because every day I get to do things that empower professional and volunteer non-profit leaders to be more successful in not just touching lives but improving and saving them. I'm inspired by the passionate people I've been lucky enough to get to know. You won't recognize many of their names, but they are true heroes. They are a varied and magnificent group of American philanthropists, people of all ages, races, places and backgrounds, and their generosity changes the world in so many ways.

This optimism undergirds my entire approach to training in which I try to instill a genuine spirit of joy. I want my love of fundraising to rub off on all those who participate in our workshops, webinars, webcasts and podcasts, and read what I have to share on resource development. But my career journey certainly didn't start with this ambition. It was decades before I ever heard of the development or fundraising profession.

Working for yourself is hugely satisfying, though I must admit it means working for the toughest boss that you will ever have. You are the brand, product, sales force, service provider and body, mind and soul of the organization all wrapped up in one. There is only one standard: Give it everything you've got.

Throughout my life, I have been fortunate to learn from a sage and generous band of mentors, supervisors, teachers, colleagues and friends. They have shared more wisdom than I could have ever wished for. I learned how to write, speak in public, conduct meetings, plan and implement PR strategies and, most importantly, how to bond with and motivate others to act.

In my mind, it makes perfect sense why I love my work as a fundraising trainer. I've always dreamed of playing a role, no matter how modest, in contributing to the greater good. This is a superb feeling to carry with you throughout the day. It's even better if you can make it your life's work.

Another bonus of my dream job is the opportunity to learn something new and keep on growing every day. Fundraising gives me the chance to do that. It's one of the most continuous improvement professions. You learn something from every interaction with a donor prospect and you learn something from each solicitation, whether the response is yes, no, or maybe.

That's why I love conversations with colleagues and all those engaged in the non-profit sector. In the truest sense we represent a giant learning community in which everyone has something meaningful to share and can enrich our perspective.

The demand for fundraising training is enormous and keeps on growing. Too many admirable non-profit leaders, who are fearless about everything else they must face in their lives, are terrified of asking for a gift for their favorite cause. (The wealthier the donor and the bigger the amount of the ask, the greater the fear.) Most of this is based on fear of the unknown. They just haven't experienced a solicitation for themselves.

Also, too many are only familiar with the passive act of getting gifts, in stark contrast to asking for gifts. Admittedly, getting gifts is better than no gifts at all, but getting and asking are quite different things. When a non-profit gets a gift, the donor completely sets the agenda of how much, when and for what purpose the gift will be used. When the non-profit asks for a gift, it can profoundly influence how much, when and for what purpose the gift will be used.

Those of us who are comfortable and actually enjoy asking for gifts don't have any superpowers. Successful fundraising is built on sound principles, proven strategies and time-tested best practices. Like everything else in life, you become better at doing it the more often you do it.

After a fulfilling career holding advancement leadership positions at three institutions of higher learning in the San Antonio area, in 2018 I took direct aim at pursuing the dream of going out on my own and becoming a fundraising trainer/consultant. It has proved to be an exciting adventure. The highlight has been leading more than 250 workshops and webinars. Collaborating with corporate sponsors including Microsoft, Texas Capital Bank, Catto & Catto and MassMutual/South Texas, led to offering empowerment workshops open to professional and volunteer non-profit leaders from organizations of all sizes and from all different sectors.

We started out by firmly embracing a concept of forming a learning community in which subject matter experts joined me in leading presentations. Perhaps the best part of these workshops was letting everyone in the audience chime in and share their experience, wisdom and insights to create the most knowledge in the aggregate. Learning can and should be interactive and fun.

Sessions typically ran 60 to 90 minutes. We

implemented a variety of formats, from Lunch and Learn, late afternoon and my personal favorite, the Happy Learning Hour. Non-profit participants were eager to learn, ask questions, share viewpoints, network and simply enjoy each other's company. In the true sense of the meaning, we are kindred spirits.

The Covid pandemic prompted a transition to the webinar format. Keep in mind, I was a complete rookie in the webinar space. We are truly fortunate to have the opportunity to collaborate with a masterful producer, John Largent, CEO of Largent Media, who guided me every step of the way. Leading experts from a wide range of disciplines essential to advancement success graciously joined us to share their immeasurable wisdom. I learned so much from every subject matter expert participating in our webinar series.

Despite the pandemic, and thanks in large part to technology, our learning community exponentially expanded in both numbers of participants and geography. It is exhilarating to add non-profit voices from across the country and even internationally, who contribute to our commitment to learn and grow together. I cherish hosting the webinars and look forward to their continuation, with an emphasis on ramping up audience participation, engagement and interaction.

Something pleasantly surprised me, too. I fell in love with the whole webinar process, from selecting topics and speakers, producing timely questions for the experts, and especially interacting with an ever-growing audience. In some ways, learning community members are vastly different, but all share an essential characteristic that I love — devotion to non-profits that are all about touching, improving and saving more lives. We want to create a world better than the one we were born into.

I enjoyed writing my first book, *10 Simple Fundraising Lessons*, which pulled together the highlights of early presentations and emphasized a central theme of common sense. In so many important ways, fundraising is intuitive. Too many times non-profit leaders overthink situations and in doing so, run amok. Simple and direct is always a more effective strategy.

In 2023, it was exciting to launch a podcast series, Nominate Your Non-Profit North Star (see page 103), to salute the personal stories of the inspiring men and women, unsung heroes, who drive the missions of their organizations steadily forward.

I've had the joy and privilege of training hundreds of non-profit leaders including many who claimed they would do anything for their non-profit except fundraising. It has been a source of immense pride to see them overcome this reluctance and emerge as effective fundraisers and propel their respective visions of good works forward. A top priority is to make our programs not only enjoyable, but actually fun.

Fundraising is part science and part art. The more you know the science, the more effective you will be in applying the art.

No one can pretend to have all the answers. I certainly don't. Think of me as your facilitator. My role is to stimulate and focus your thinking on the elements that culminate in gifts to your non-profit. A critical component is prompting lively discussions within your organizations. That's why each chapter of this book concludes with a set of homework assignments that hopefully you will not perform individually but will address as a non-profit team or committee.

As a leader you are intimately familiar with what your non-profit means to others and the community. It matters! You know that your programs, employees and especially beneficiaries deserve the best. By actively participating in fundraising processes, you will be taking concrete action in ensuring that your non-profit reaches its full potential. You can even achieve the most prized gifts of all — leadership gifts of $1 million or more!

Now, let's address the all-important "how?"

What Is a Major Gift?

A "major gift" means different amounts to different organizations and can even mean different amounts to the same organization, depending on where they are in their history.

One size doesn't fit all. In other words, you can ask 10 respected non-profit leaders, and quickly hear 10 different answers that are all based on credible rationale.

This much is clear and consistent among the nation's 1.5 million non-profits: Without an effective major gifts strategy, the organization is going to fall short of successfully advancing its essential mission without the resources it deserves. In other words, major gifts will make or break the success of any fundraising program.

Not long ago, research showed that about 88% of total gift income came from just 12% of the donors. But in today's era of billionaire mega-donors, many experts are now estimating the split may be closer to 90%+ to 10%+ Or even 95% to 5%.

Another reality we can't ignore is that an estimated 88% of our nation's non-profits have annual budgets of $500,000 or less. This means that, to many organizations, a major gift as modest as $10,000 can achieve major impact. More established and sophisticated development departments might easily place the standard at $100,000 or more.

Then, as the late Jerold Panas — arguably the most admired fundraising authority of our time — asserted, it is the donor, not the non-profit, that decides what and how much a major gift is.

Putting together and implementing a major gifts initiative doesn't have to be complex or burdensome. It doesn't have to be expensive. The chief requirement is the time commitment made by non-profit leaders to initiate, nurture, and sustain personal relationships that culminate in lifetime friendships and gifts. The conviction and passion of solicitors will influence results more than elaborate print, video and digital collateral material.

Every non-profit has an inner circle of supporters and friends that make your organization their top philanthropic priority and are willing to back up that conviction with their gifts of time and money. They must play crucial roles in the discovery, cultivation, solicitation and stewardship of major gift donors, especially million-dollar donors.

Major gifts, leadership gifts, principal gifts and other descriptors fill the vocabulary of the fundraising profession. Again, they will all have different meanings and different numbers to illustrate them.

This is why I prefer to rely on the standard of million-dollar gifts. There is absolute clarity on what the goal is and how success is measured. I strongly believe every non-profit, especially smaller and mid-size operations, should be thinking in terms of obtaining its first or next million-dollar gift. The timing couldn't be better. The money is out there, and societal needs are overwhelmingly compelling. American philanthropy awards those non-profits who convincingly request support at a pace of about $1 million a minute.

If I were to pay $1 million to purchase your home, despite all other variables, that is precisely what your home would be worth. It's the same in the world of fundraising. Once you receive your first million-dollar gift your non-profit suddenly becomes an organization that is viewed by donors and prospects as a non-profit worthy of seven-figure gifts.

Receiving your first million-dollar gift completely changes how your non-profit is viewed both internally and externally. Suddenly everyone believes that more is possible. And it is!

So let's focus on the art and science of obtaining your first or next million-dollar gift.

Homework

- Study your database: What are the largest gifts you've received?
- What are the stories and motivations behind those largest gifts?
- How prestigious and influential are your largest donors?
- Who are the donors in the tier of gifts right below the highest level? What are the prospects for requesting and achieving increases?
- Who can board members introduce and break the ice to as prospective major gift donors?

Mission Possible

Every fundraising initiative — whether it's to advance annual giving, planned giving, endowment, capital campaigns or a major gifts program — starts with your non-profit's mission. A clear and sharp mission statement serves to guide all major decisions that a non-profit will be challenged to make — especially decisions about which new programs and projects to undertake, which to avoid, and which to exit. You should put substantial effort into revisiting your mission, vision and values. It is more than well worth the time.

We've always lived in a world of constant change, but now those changes are on steroids, particularly made so by the pandemic. So, gather your management, staff, board and other key stakeholders to have a frank discussion of your mission, vision and values that serve as guideposts for everything that you want to do to succeed. Just in case the participants aren't clear on this agenda, let's quickly review some definitions:

- **Mission** defines what the organization does.
- **Vision** defines what the organization aspires to be.
- **Values** tell us what the organization believes in.

These three critical components should be reviewed on an ongoing basis and the need for a piercing review has never been so important. Always keep this reality in front of you: Donors are faced with making difficult choices on how to invest finite resources of time and money. They are not choosing between the good and the bad but choosing between the good and the good. Think hard and honestly and assess both your strengths and weaknesses. A common shortcoming is a mission statement that is too broad. Tighten your focus as you address the following critical questions:

What makes your organization distinctive? How does it stand out from all others like it?

How do you contribute to improving the quality of life in ways that all the other fine non-profits can't?

What would be the consequences if your organization didn't exist?

Now is the time to make sure your case for support (a cogent appeal to donor prospects grounded in the mission) and key messaging empowers your organization to compete and succeed in the competitive fundraising environment.

Mission, vision and values need to drive another crucial function. They serve as a potent force that rallies together the board, staff, donors, volunteers and other supporters during good times and not-so-good times. They unite people who will invariably have differences of opinion on lesser matters and instead see the big picture of expansive vision and desired outcomes.

I'm also a strong advocate of simple and concise strategic plans. I've seen too many non-profits spend far too long on developing complex strategic plans that never get off the bookshelf. Frankly, mammoth strategic plans are seldom realistic. They typically go far beyond the bandwidth that staff, board, volunteers and supporters can achieve.

When it comes to strategic plans, less is more. Start by reaching agreement on three overarching goals for the upcoming year. Then overlay your strategies and tactics to bring these goals to fruition. If you accomplish all of them early, you'll be in the enviable position of adding a new goal to the list. Your mission, vision and values can also set the stage for core marketing messages to be highlighted through every communications channel available, whether it is print, electronic or digital.

As my sage friend and colleague, Marv LeRoy, President and Founder of the Institute for Philanthropic Excellence, likes to put it: More Money = More Mission. When it comes to defining your mission, adopt a "bumper sticker" mindset. Your statement should be so basic and easy to understand that the board and staff can easily commit it to memory. Always keep in mind that money is not the end. It is a means to the end and ramping up your organization's capacity to play a leadership role in making the world a better place to live through your mission.

Homework

- When was your mission, vision and values last updated?
- Do you consider your mission, vision and values still timely?
- How distinctive and different is your mission, vision and values from other organizations?
- Who has the requisite skills and background to lead a productive revisiting of your mission, vision and values? Do you need to bring in an outside facilitator?
- How can you test your updated mission, vision and values with donors and prospective donors?

The Gift Cycle

The principles, strategies, and best practices for successful resource development really aren't that different for earning $1,000 gifts and $1 million gifts.

You identify those most likely to be interested in your mission and contribute time and money. You cultivate interest with compelling stories and opportunities to see the mission in action. You set the stage for a successful solicitation. You thank donors sincerely and enthusiastically, so you can come back the next year and ask them to give again and even consider increasing their level of support.

As I explained in my book *10 Simple Fundraising Lessons*, I like organizing major gift initiatives around the four distinct parts of the gift cycle:

Discovery: What are the donor prospect's values, priorities and interests?

Cultivation: What are you doing to forge a personal and emotional bond?

Solicitation: When, how much, and for what are you asking?

Stewardship: What are you doing to thank donors for the last gift?

Let's take a closer look at each of these phases.

Discovery: Who Will Give?

The discovery process begins with the identification of those most likely to give. Who should you consider approaching for support? To identify these donors, you can use what I call the "CIA Prospect Identification System": C= Capacity, I= Inclination, A= Access.

Capacity is what usually comes to mind first when you start searching for prospects. It identifies someone's financial ability to make a gift, driven by their income and wealth. I often see non-profit ears perk up when hearing that so-and-so has a lot of money. Of course, there can be several significant nuances to this information, such as liquidity, financial commitments, and family pressures. Too much emphasis can be placed on wealth indicating a hot prospect. Remember, just because someone is wealthy doesn't mean they're going to give to your organization or cause.

Inclination is where you start to dig deeper and understand motivations. If the donor prospect is wealthy, do you know if he or she is philanthropic and has demonstrated this by donating to charitable causes? And, if that person is philanthropic, why do you believe he or she will care about *your* cause? The philanthropic landscape is fiercely competitive. You should have a strong rationale to conclude that a donor prospect has a genuine connection to the cause or could be cultivated to develop such an interest.

Access is your biggest hurdle. Even if you can establish capacity and inclination, you still must figure out how you're going to be able to approach the donor prospect. Usually, the bigger the donor, the tougher the challenge. This is where board members, volunteers and friends of the organization can and should play a huge role. By serving as connectors and breaking the ice, they can contribute mightily to resource development success without ever actually asking for a gift. The "Six Degrees of Separation" theory reminds us that everyone on the planet is separated by no more than six personal relationships. (In some communities, it's more like two degrees of separation.) You and members of your organization are no more than six relationships removed from any donor prospect in the world. The collective reach of personal and professional networks is enormous. And don't overlook the value of your database and those who have been loyally supporting you over the years. It's a good bet that you have major gift donors among their ranks.

Cultivation: Clearing the Path to "Yes"

Think of the process that culminates in a gift as a continuum that begins with "Hello, nice to meet you" and concludes with "Thank you for your gift of $1 million." Experts note that about 90 percent of our work precedes the solicitation, so the stage must be properly set. If in real estate, it's location, location, location, in fundraising — especially major gift work — it's cultivation, cultivation, cultivation. Cultivation is about forging a personal and emotional bond, which isn't that complicated. It's helping the prospective donor develop a deep appreciation of the mission your organization serves. More specifically, it's about conveying what needs your organization addresses that aren't being addressed by any other organization.

Cultivation can take a variety of forms. The initial outreach needs to help you discover interests, values, and priorities. As the relationship develops, it's fitting that you introduce prospects to your organization's leadership, get them on-site so they see your facilities and programs close up, and see for themselves how you touch and improve lives. (We've learned that virtual tours can suffice.)

A simple cultivation plan should be developed outlining steps that will introduce the donor prospect to the mission so that when he or she is asked for the gift, the answer will be favorable and at the level requested. The larger the amount being requested, the more time needs to be devoted to cultivation.

We need to methodically connect with the heart and head and find a genuine fit with the prospect. Fundraising demands the talents of asking the right questions and being an active listener. Ask probing questions and listen closely, and the donor will tell you when, how much and for what to ask for.

Solicitation: Enjoying the Ask

If the discovery and cultivation phases have been done properly, the time is ready to ask for the gift. This should be something that everyone enjoys. Although many board members and volunteers might be uncomfortable asking for the gift, that doesn't have to be an impediment. Other board members and especially staff can step up and handle that task. But it's important that the board member or volunteer who has the relationship with the prospect be present for the solicitation.

Marketing materials rarely influence major gift donors to say "yes." In fact, handing them a printed proposal should be delayed until the request has been made, and then it should be left behind to speak for the organization and project when you are no longer present. What is more effective is the unbridled passion of the solicitor. Collateral material must be first-class, but success hinges much more on the ability to secure appointments, and then making the best possible use of that precious time.

Stewardship: The Right and Smart Thing to Do

Stewardship is an extension of cultivation, coming after the gift has been received. Thoughtfully acknowledging and thanking donors for their gifts is crucial. It's a proven way to get donors to do what we want them to do next — give again, give again sooner, and give more.

Keep in mind that donors rarely begin by making leadership gifts of $1 million. Instead, they prefer to kick the tires first, and start by making a modest gift. Then they watch the results your organization can deliver on that investment and how they are treated by leadership, board and staff. In this spirit, your non-profit needs to commit to developing a pipeline of major gift donors who start small but by effective cultivation and stewardship can be motivated to continually upgrade their gifts because they feel such increases have been earned.

A smart guide is The Rule of 7X. Every gift should be acknowledged, and the donor thanked seven distinct times during the year. This might take different forms — a letter, a phone call, a private lunch, a public event involving many donors (which can be virtual), an article in a publication, a story on your website, and so on. (My personal favorite is a handwritten thank you note.) But whatever you do, never include a solicitation appeal in a thank you letter or other stewardship activity.

Having board members make random thank you calls to donors is not only a high value stewardship practice but also a smart way to introduce reluctant individuals to the fundraising process. The call might result in voice-mail messages being left, but it will still make a strong impression.

For as long as we can remember, face-to-face meetings have been the gold standard in fundraising, especially when pursuing major gifts. The fundraising environment was turned upside down in 2020 by the realities of a pandemic and social distancing. Fortunately, we discovered that virtual fundraising such as videoconferencing can work in the discovery, cultivation, solicitation and stewardship of donors and donor prospects. Virtual fundraising has even demonstrated concrete results in securing leadership gifts of seven and eight figures. With social distancing requirements being unnecessary, the pace of face-to-face interaction is being restored. But whether it's an in-person, virtual, or hybrid approach, major gifts initiatives will produce exciting results for the non-profits that embrace the art and science of fundraising.

Homework

- How do you identify new prospects?
- What are your most effective ways to cultivate prospects and introduce them to the mission?
- Who on your board and staff genuinely enjoys asking for gifts?
- How are donors acknowledged and thanked for their last gift?
- How do you communicate with donors and prospects to keep them informed of challenges and opportunities facing the organization?

Friendships Over Relationships

In the movie, "He's Just Not That Into You," there's a memorable line defining relationships as something you have until something better comes along. This reminds me that we use the word "relationship" way too much in the fundraising business and other professions, too. I'm not going to worry about the other professions, but to secure precious gifts of time and money, fundraisers need to dig deeper and work harder to obtain an association that is based on common values, priorities and interests, so both parties come out ahead. Donors are not to be viewed and treated as ATM machines.

Your goal is establishing a true friendship that draws donor prospects closer and closer to your organization, its mission, the staff, board and volunteers, and the beneficiaries of their gifts. Over time, it should grow deeper, more personal and more meaningful. In fact, the test of that friendship, in contrast to a mere relationship, is that it can sustain a solicitation that is turned down, and the donor and the non-profit continue a steady stream of communication about the mission of the organization that binds them together.

And this friendship isn't just one dimensional. Both the donor and the non-profit derive benefits.

People in the fundraising profession should welcome opportunities to speak and interact with donor prospects when there is no discussion of money and gifts at all. This is when the bonding can happen in a relaxed setting.

Always be on the lookout for ways in which you can help your donors. A splendid example during the pandemic was assisting donors to become more comfortable with new technologies such as videoconferencing. Many major donors are seniors and are not as familiar with modern technologies as younger generations. By helping them learn videoconferencing, we not only strengthen their relationship with the non-profit, but open the door for them to have stronger relationships with family members, especially children and grandchildren.

An always tricky question is, what gifts should non-profits give donors to convey appreciation for their support? I strongly believe that donors don't need or want more "stuff." They have less and less room to store trophies, plaques and other gift mementos, and are looking to lighten their inventory of these presents from non-profits. Many donors also resent money being spent on elaborate gifts.

I'm a strong advocate of much more personal touches. Try sharing digital images of how donors are making a difference in propelling the non-profit's mission forward. If they are so inclined, they can print images to display. But in the interest of saving time, if they want to share them, they will probably just e-mail the images to family members and friends.

When soliciting million-dollar gifts you are sure to run into the challenge of power imbalances in which the donor is in a much stronger position of wealth, prestige and visibility. Both the donor and solicitor are going to be challenged to rise above this reality and recognize that the value of a change agent, especially a friend, means as much as wealth and power.

Another advantage of the friendship perspective is that it is common for friends to make introductions to other friends. Just like a friend is going to tell someone about a new restaurant they particularly enjoyed, a friend is going to tell a friend about a non-profit of which they are fond. Right after they make a gift, and their emotions are running high, is a great time to ask if they have friends with similar interests who might be interested in learning about the non-profit.

Homework

- How often do you communicate with donors — via in-person, snail mail, text, telephone, e-mail video-conferencing or social media? And do you know their communication preferences?
- How are responsibilities assigned to staff and board for staying in touch with donors?
- Who are some of your donors who have provided support the longest?
- Interview long-time donors on what they enjoy most about their affiliation with the organization.
- What services and support can you provide donors during challenging times like when the pandemic hit?

Gifts From Individuals Rule

Over the past several decades, so many things have changed in the world of philanthropy and some are of major significance. But one especially important characteristic hasn't changed at all: The sources of American generosity. *Giving USA* has been tracking philanthropy sources and recipients since 1956 and finds that gifts from individuals consistently account for about two-thirds of overall giving.

Now, I love gifts from foundations and corporations as much as the next person, but I contend that you should go fishing where the fish are biting. And in philanthropy, most of the fish are biting in the pool of gifts from individuals. In fact, when you factor in bequests and gifts from family foundations, this share rises to a whopping 85%+.

Another favorable characteristic is that individuals tend to reach decisions more quickly than corporations and foundations.

For these reasons, whenever I work with non-profits on developing prospect lists, I like to see the lists populated by a majority of individual philanthropists.

Giving decisions are driven by the heart and the brain. The brain asks challenging questions like: How do you measure the impact of our gift? What type of recognition will we receive? Can't you work with a smaller amount? The heart will ask more emotional questions such as: How can I help? How can we turn up the volume? What are the most effective solutions to the problems we are addressing?

None of this is to suggest that it is easy to obtain gifts from individual philanthropists. But I fervently recommend that major gift programs highlight the cultivation of individuals.

What motivates individuals to give? There has been plenty of research conducted on this critically important question. Ask a group of experts and you'll get several different responses, prioritized in different sequences.

But here are my thoughts based on my career as practitioner and consultant.

1. They were asked. It doesn't get more fundamental than that. But it makes a huge difference who does the asking. Donors prefer to contribute to people and causes that they know, like and trust. It typically takes time to earn such trust. This much is for certain — if you don't ask, you don't get.

2. The solicitation is made in person, if not eyeball-to- eyeball, screen-to-screen. Foundation Center research found:

- When asked face-to-face, 70% will give at a rate of 50% the amount requested.
- When asked during a phone call, 25% will give at a rate of 25% the amount requested.
- When asked by mail, about 2% will give gifts of $10 to $25.

3. Money follows time. The more time a donor prospect gives to learn about the non-profit, the more likely he or she is to make a gift, especially a leadership gift of $1 million. The strongest example applies to volunteers. Americans who volunteer their time and skills to non-profits donate an average of 10 times more money to charity than people who don't volunteer, according to a comprehensive national study by the Fidelity® Charitable Gift Fund and VolunteerMatch.

4. The mission is personal. The donor prospect has been either personally touched by the organization, or a loved one has been touched. Prime examples include alumni giving back to their alma maters, or grateful patients who have either been saved or treated themselves or have had loved ones saved or treated by health care facilities.

5. They are "wowed" by the timely impact and results of the non-profit. This often happens in response to emergencies and disasters. This is typically expedited by massive news coverage and publicity.

6. It runs in the family. Many wealthy individuals grow up with an affinity for causes that their parents, grandparents and other family members made a high priority. In some cases there can be an aura of prestige associated with a non-profit.

7. They are inspired by the leadership of the organization. This could be a charismatic CEO or board chair who activates a magnetic pull to the non-profit.

8. They appreciate tax benefits. There is a good reason I place this at the end of the list. Sure, wealthy individuals like taking tax deductions, but the truth is any of the nation's 1.5 million non-profits can offer tax benefits, so this is hardly a distinguishing factor.

No doubt, you can add to this list. You can reframe the text or change the order of priority. But I will strongly argue that each plays a significant role in influencing leadership donors to make their gifts.

Homework

- What is your distribution of gift income among these sources — individuals, bequests, corporations and foundations?

- Visit your leading individual donors and ask them for referrals to friends they think would be interested in the mission of the non-profit.
- How are the stories of leading individual donors highlighted through available communication channels?
- Consider celebrating "donor-versaries" marking milestones of providing support for one, five, 10 years or more.
- Be sure you have introduced the organization to the next generation in the families of major gift donors in their senior years.

Stretching Amounts

Embrace the attitude that you and the donor sit on the same side of the table. You share a passion for making the mission of the organization or the goal of the project achieve its greatest potential. There are many financial strategies and tactics that can empower the donor to give more, some of them without reaching into cash resources. It is your job to understand these options and explain them in clear terms that the donor prospect can easily understand so that eventually they can choose to take advantage of them. In many cases financial institutions and advisors will enthusiastically collaborate with you to help donors better understand the power of these tools.

A traditional approach is giving donors the ability to stretch their gifts through multi-year pledges.

Million-dollar gifts are seldom paid as a lump sum but paid over a pledge period such as three to five years. The larger the amount, the longer the pledge period likely will be. Incidentally, many million-dollar donors like the appeal of challenge gifts that amplify their impact by triggering the generosity of others.

There are several other practical tactics to consider.

Make monthly giving easy and visible. Erica Waasdorp, President, A Direct Solution, who has been a guest on our webinars several times, highlights enormous returns on minimal investment — more giving, higher retention, and doors opening to major and planned gifts, to name a few.

Also, make sure Donor Advised Funds (DAFs) are visible on your website, in your marketing material, and during solicitations. This is the most dynamic component of American philanthropy. The National Philanthropic Trust 2023 Donor-Advised Fund Report, the most comprehensive data on the state of donor-advised fund philanthropy in the U.S., shows that the value of DAF grantmaking to charitable organizations increased 9% to $52 billion and the number of accounts grew 2.9% to approximately two million.

Another proven tactic is to bundle together gifts from family members and close friends. This makes perfect sense when the purpose of the gift has strong appeal across generations. It opens the door to keep on building the size of an endowment or other project over time. And it also provides a wonderful way to bring families closer together through shared philanthropic aspirations.

A long-time robust component of leadership giving — spurred by the pandemic that reinforced the reality that we are all mortal — planned giving has become more popular than ever. The most popular forms are charitable bequests, retirement plans, and insurance policies. Legacy gifts provide powerful tools to significantly increase the size of the gift while postponing any out-of-pocket expenditure. Typically, a donor can give several times as much from their estate than they can from income and current wealth position. Search your database for consistent repeat annual donors; they don't necessarily have to give large gifts. They often make good candidates for planned giving appeals.

Finally, in this historically robust stock market, many of your donors are likely holding enormously appreciated assets. Donating these stocks to their favorite non-profits can help them avoid costly capital gains taxes. Higher stock prices and home values drove an 8% gain in 2023 net worth, so assets like stocks and real estate — not cash — are more likely to fuel major gifts.

Homework

- For starters, ask donors if they have included your non-profit in their estate plans. You would be surprised how many may have done so but have not informed you.

- How strong is your network of financial and investment advisors who can provide expertise on estate planning, gifts of stocks, DAFs and other remunerative giving methods?
- Do you have a recognition society for those including the non-profit in their estate plans?
- How do you share stories that illustrate that a wide range of donors — not just the very wealthy — can make planned giving gifts?
- Have you challenged your board of directors to lead by example and include the non-profit in their estate plans?

Asking: In Person and Virtually

For as long as we can remember, meeting with donors — especially when asking for major gifts — was best done face-to-face. Many seasoned fundraising professionals find it hard to believe that major gifts can be solicited any other way. But just like social distancing changed almost everything else, fundraising was forced to adapt and change. We are even seeing hybrid solicitations in which some non-profit leaders meet in person with the prospect, while others participate through videoconferencing.

Here's good news: There are plenty of encouraging results from the virtual discovery, cultivation, solicitation and stewardship of gifts, including major gifts. Some of our best practices remain absolutely the same, while necessity requires others to change. Consider this a blending of the best practices from in-person solicitations with the advantages of virtual communication.

Asking is at the very heart of such successful fundraising. We want to present a detailed step-by-step description of a winning solicitation. Here are 10 general tips to help you make the most of both opportunities to effectively ask for $1 million in-person or virtually.

(1) Start with a strong relationship. This is the foundation of any solicitation, no matter the format. A major gift ask requires sustained cultivation to sufficiently inform, engage and inspire the donor prospect to consider making a substantial investment. A million-dollar gift typically requires vigorous efforts to boldly heighten the donor prospect's appreciation of the mission, programs, leadership and impact.

If relying on virtual communication, make sure the donor is entirely comfortable with the technology being used. It may be necessary to conduct a practice run focusing on informal conversation to ensure things will run smoothly.

(2) Schedule a time that works best for the donor. Everyone is different, so your flexibility is at a premium. If you're the host, get online several minutes before the donor is invited. (Don't forget to pay close attention to time zones.)

(3) Don't overwhelm the prospect. A good rule of thumb is that there should be no more than twice the number of solicitors than prospects. So if you're soliciting one prospect, be sure there are no more than two of you. A combination of one

volunteer (particularly if they enjoy a relationship with the prospect) and one staff member works well. Also, try to manage the video call so the prospect is speaking to only one solicitor at a time and there are only two primary images on the screen. It's important to consider that virtual solicitations are generally more tiring and should last no longer than half to two-thirds of the time spent in a face-to-face meeting.

Admittedly, I'm a time management freak and am always afraid of running out of time. Time management demands discipline, and the solicitor must find a tactful way to oversee it. Consider this time sequence:

• Five minutes (maximum): Opening pleasantries. For some this may appear to be counter-intuitive, but how you start the meeting will set the tone of how serious you are about managing time.

• Five minutes: Presentation of the problem or challenge being addressed.

• Five minutes: Compelling arguments on how the request responds to the problem/ challenge.

• Two minutes: The ask.

• 15-20 minutes: Responding to questions/ concerns.

• Five minutes: Wrap-up/next steps (especially setting a good time for a follow-up visit or call).

Laura Fredericks, JD, The Expert on the ASK, and my go-to expert on all matters fundraising, suggests a 75%/25% formula in which the donor prospect talks 75% of the time and the solicitor 25%. That is a vivid reminder that the solicitor must make the very best use of every minute he or she is speaking.

(4) Always ask for a specific amount. We live in a price-tag-driven world, and philanthropy is no different. Highlight the rationale on how the amount was determined. The solicitor will not have credibility unless he or she has made a stretch gift themselves. I don't worry as much as others do about under-asking, because if you do a good job of stewardship you can go back and ask for more..

(5) Be ready for questions, most of which will focus on these four areas:

- The Organization
- The Project
- The Amount
- The Timing

(6) You may want to present a few strategic and compelling images. Keep these to an absolute minimum, and use text, facts and numbers sparingly.

(7) After the ask is made, remain silent. Even if this seems like an eternity, resist the temptation to say anything until the prospect has responded. Too many gifts are lost or reduced by failing to adhere to this principle. This is a good reason why

we have two people on the solicitation end, so that the person who makes the "ask" can comfortably remain quiet, and the other person can intercede if the pause becomes too lengthy.

(8) Leave-behind material should be used exactly that way. Never ask the prospect to read along with the proposal as you review high points since you never want to jeopardize eyeball-to-eyeball contact, in person or over the computer screen. For virtual meetings, you can send material electronically to speak for you after the meeting has been concluded.

(9) Close with authority. If you're fortunate enough to receive a "yes," thank profusely. Often, the prospect may ask for more time. If so, this is crucial: Set a specific date and time to conduct another meeting or video call to resume the conversation. Even if the prospect says "no," thank them for their time and suggest you would like to stay in contact to keep them apprised of progress.

By the way, if we do a good job with cultivation, we seldom hear "no." However, we might hear back, "not for that project," "not for that amount," and/or "not at this time." Always seek to end the conversation on a positive note, especially if it's a request to meet again with a re-crafted proposal.

(10) Follow-up with both an e-mail summary of what was discussed and next steps and send a

handwritten thank you note. The handwritten note is regarded as the secret sauce in the fundraising recipe. How many handwritten notes do you receive? It will make you stand out. Send a note even if you're turned down. There may be a more opportune occasion to solicit the same donor prospect in the future.

Homework

- What type of preparation goes into a major gift solicitation? Have you rehearsed?
- What kind of debriefing is conducted following a solicitation, honestly assessing the positives and negatives?
- How do you ensure immediate follow-up to a solicitation?
- How is progress on prospects monitored, tracked and evaluated?
- How do you share stories that illustrate that a wide range of donors — not just the very wealthy — can make planned giving gifts?

It Takes a Non-Profit Village

Early in the year I was contacted by a friend of a non-profit, who said that the organization could benefit from my services as a fundraising trainer/ consultant. Referrals are the lifeblood of any good consultant's practice.

I dutifully followed up with the non-profit CEO. He replied that the organization didn't have the time to commit to board and staff training because he was in financial quicksand and desperately needed "a quick fix."

The situation was exacerbated not just by the lack of willingness to commit to fees, but the CEO wasn't even interested in receiving our free monthly e-newsletter and invitations to free webinars featuring experts from throughout the advancement arena.

Of course I was disappointed by the response, but it also reinforced my conviction that there aren't any quick fixes for non-profits who want to secure long-term financial health and viability.

It takes time, serious commitment and — to paraphrase an expression — the support of an entire non-profit village. Every staff member, board member and volunteer can and should contribute to the advancement of the non-profit through the discovery, cultivation, solicitation and stewardship of donor prospects. Everything occurring in the life of the non-profit is a potential cultivation opportunity.

Quick fixes just don't work and typically place non-profits in the inevitable position of falling deeper and deeper into financial holes. No single dynamic staff member, board member, brilliant PR campaign or even one magnanimous donor can lift a non-profit from financial hardship to solvency. It takes building a genuine culture of philanthropy in which all stakeholders recognize a personal responsibility for the implementation of sound fundraising processes.

It doesn't matter if you have an aversion to asking for gifts, since there are many other ways to concretely advance resource development results. You can identify prospective donors, break the ice and introduce prospects to the mission of the organization, proudly share stories, accomplishments and key messages, and thank all those who contribute precious gifts of time and money.

All too often non-profits fall into the trap of thinking there is a singular development professional, who they view like a lone gunfighter, who has a portfolio of rich contacts which can be conveniently converted into major gift donors.

It just doesn't work that way. In fact, placing unreasonable expectations on new staff without providing them with the infrastructure and support necessary to succeed is a major reason that there is so much churn and turnover in the development profession. The sad reality is that a non-profit is lucky if it can keep a good development officer for two years. The higher the immediate expectations and the severity of financial problems, the more likely staff retention will be limited to a shorter period. This culminates in a vicious cycle in which a non-profit is continuously searching for and replacing staff, frustrating donor prospects who must work with people who aren't familiar with their philanthropic vision and personality.

As a trainer, I must admit to having a vested interest in organizations that are willing to commit the time and resources to build a culture of philanthropy from the ground up. I like to train board and staff members as an advancement team, because after I leave they must work together as a team if they are to be successful in nurturing relationships and asking for and receiving gifts of time and money.

Even one very generous donor doesn't have the power to magically turn around a financially weak organization. Sure, their infusion of much-needed capital will resuscitate the organization for a while, but inevitably the benefit will end. Every donor deserves to know how the organization will sustain its momentum and impact once their gift dollars run out.

Fundraising training must get across that resource development isn't something to fear like a root canal or a colorectal exam. Instead, we emphasize that it is primarily an extension of the passion that professional and volunteer non-profit leaders have for their respective organizations.

My training extends far beyond classroom lectures, whether in person or virtual. It emphasizes hands-on learning exercises such as practicing elevator pitches, identifying prospects from personal, professional and civic networks and, most importantly, rehearsing and role playing the ask. The biggest reason that most people are afraid of asking for money is that they just haven't seen or experienced a genuine solicitation for themselves.

Anyone who works or volunteers for a non-profit recognizes that its programs, employees, and especially beneficiaries, deserve the best.

Fundraising is part science and part art. The better you know science, the more skillfully you can practice the art.

I wholeheartedly reject the notion that fundraisers are born and not made. The idea that some people can't take the rejection is unrealistic. You can't succeed in any career path or endeavor without risking failure and particularly hearing the word "no." Hardly a day goes by in which I don't hear no several times. We come to appreciate that it is never personal.

As I've emphasized before, there are 1.5 million non-profits in this country serving a wide range of timely missions and improving the quality of life in essential areas such as healthcare, education, economic development, childcare, seniors, arts and culture, animal welfare and others. The ones that succeed and flourish embrace a long-term view and are in the forever business. They are going to prudently invest in the people, infrastructure, training and other resources that will empower them to face challenges today and tomorrow.

I'm about as far from unbiased as you can get, but I don't think there's a better investment of finite time and resources than holistically investing in providing everyone affiliated with your non-profit with the knowledge, skills and especially the confident mindset that they can and should play an active role in advancing the success of the non-profit through the multi-faceted fundraising processes.

Homework

- How are non-fundraising staff members encouraged to contribute to the advancement of the non-profit?
- What kind of professional development opportunities are offered to the fundraising staff?
- What kind of fundraising training is provided to board members?
- How has the staff and board been given both the technology and training to become facile in the use of videoconferencing and new media?
- How do you recognize and celebrate successful solicitations?

Million-Dollar Conversations

Most people are scared of asking for gifts in any amount. With that attitude, asking for gifts of a million dollars or more can be downright terrifying.

There can be the perception of a significant imbalance of power. The million-dollar donor has it all because they can choose any one of 1.5 million non-profits to enrich with their generosity. More than likely, they are multi-millionaires and have led extremely successful careers and are used to getting what they want out of life.

I counsel professional and volunteer non-profit leaders to emphasize authenticity. Sorry, this might sound like advice you received for going on your first date: Just be yourself.

Better yet, be the eyes and ears — and especially the voice — of the noble cause you represent. Consider that your superpower. You can partner with the million-dollar donor to accomplish something awesome in making a difference in the world.

Most people outside of the profession also think fundraisers need to be very adept at the art of speaking, glib and persuasive. Make no mistake about it, successful fundraisers need to be excellent communicators — both orally and in writing. But I place the art of active listening at the very top of the fundraiser's must-have skill set. This culminates in being liked, known and, most importantly, trusted by the donor prospect.

All personality types can be effective solicitors. My good friend, colleague and webinar guest, Brian Saber, President of Asking Matters, a self-professed introvert, documents in his groundbreaking book, *Fundraising for Introverts*, that introverts enjoy the advantages of heightened listening and sensitivity towards other people.

In a nutshell, if we can hold enough quality conversations with donor prospects, they will tell us how much, when and for what purpose they will share their gifts of time and money. Remember the bigger the amount of the solicitation the longer the period of cultivation and engagement must be with the donor.

Listening demonstrates that we value and are genuinely interested in what the other party is thinking. What is active listening? Most people confuse passive hearing with listening to someone. There is a big difference, and donors can quickly and thoroughly sense it.

Based on hundreds of meetings and solicitations with donor prospects, here are my Top Ten recommendations on being an effective active listener, particularly when working with donors that you want to consider making a first or next million-dollar gift to your non-profit.

(1) Enter every meeting with the top agenda item being to learn as much as possible about the donor. What are their values, interests and priorities? Any discussion of money should be left for much later down the road, after a solid relationship (no, make that a solid *friendship*) has been clearly developed.

(2) Watch for nonverbal clues and reactions that count much more than words. Dr. Albert Mehrabian from UCLA's Department of Psychology, and author of *Silent Messages*, concluded that the relative impact of messages is 7% verbal, 38% vocal and 55% visual. For this reason alone, it is essential to maintain uninterrupted eye contact throughout the meeting. You need to be on the alert for all body and facial gestures. If you're lucky enough to be in their home or office, look for clues like photos, books and personal mementos which will reveal strong clues into their personalities.

(3) I understand that many people like to take notes to capture the highlights of the meeting. But for you to maintain that all-important eye contact

with the donor, I suggest that you designate a second non-profit representative at the meeting to serve as the scribe. If you are by yourself, then craft your notes immediately after you leave the donor.

(4) Many of the same rules apply for virtual communication, primarily via videoconferencing. Instead of eyeball-to-eyeball contact, it is essential to effectively maintain a similar connection through screen-to-screen contact. Virtual meetings tend to be much more exhausting than in-person, so plan them to be about one-half to two-thirds the duration of an in-person meeting.

(5) Probe for meaning. If you don't fully understand what the donor means, ask them to expand and clarify their messages.

(6) I don't care how much work has gone into your collateral material, or how attractive it is. Don't ask the donor to follow along as you review its highlights. Marketing material should be presented at the conclusion of the meeting and speak for the non-profit when your representatives are no longer present.

(7) Your questions play a huge role in deepening your understanding. Go in with a carefully crafted and honed list. Here are some of my favorite questions that will help you discover the donor's values, priorities and interests:

- What has been your most satisfying philanthropic experience? And why?

- What do you remember about your first gift to a non-profit, both good and bad?
- Putting the topic of money aside, what changes would you like to see our non-profit make happen?
- If you could be our CEO for a day, what would you concentrate on?
- A year from now, how would you be able to tell that your gift to us was a prudent investment?
- What are some of your favorite non-profits?
- How do you prefer that we communicate with you?
- How do you prefer to be recognized for your gifts?
- What do you think is the most pressing challenge facing our community?
- This question might not be suitable for all meetings: Would you be comfortable with us making a solicitation at our next meeting?

(8) Even if the donor can and should be speaking most of the time, it is the fundraiser's responsibility to manage time. (In my experience, we always seem to run out of it.) It might very well be necessary for the fundraiser to steer the conversation to a different topic, by saying something like: We would like to hear more about your opinions on subject X.

(9) Close the meeting on a high note by

repeating areas of agreement and recap next steps, particularly the timing of the next meeting if an ask hasn't been brought to closure.

(10) As soon as possible e-mail a summary of the meeting demonstrating how soundly you were listening to the donor and understanding their perspective. My personal favorite is also sending a brief handwritten note thanking the donor for their time. This will enable you to really stand out.

Million-dollar gifts are made every day. They are the culmination of working hard and working smart. You know that the mission and work of your non-profit matters. Your organization — including the staff, board, volunteers, and especially the programs and services you provide to those in need — deserve the best. There is nothing like the exhilaration of a non-profit receiving the first or next million-dollar gift that you so richly deserve. It is equally if not more exciting for the donor to make the first million-dollar gift in the life of a non-profit.

This journey starts with your conviction in the difference your non-profit makes in improving the world. By embracing the principles, strategies and best practices of the art and science of fundraising, first and next million-dollar gifts are waiting for you.

Homework

- Speak to those closest to you and honestly assess your strengths and weaknesses.
- Design and implement a personal improvement program to strengthen your areas of weakness.
- Think about your organization's top donors and prospects. How do your personalities align?
- You may not be the best match for some of these top donors and prospects. If so, they should be assigned to another professional or volunteer leader of the organization.
- Do you feel you have the confidence and skill set to speak to individuals who are much more prosperous and successful than you are? This is a requirement.

It Starts and Ends with Ethics

Every profession likes to claim ethics are essential to its success. But you can make an especially cogent argument that this is indeed the case in fundraising.

What does it take to be successful in fundraising? Strengths like persuasion, problem-solving and persistence come quickly to mind. But integrity is squarely at the top.

Fundraising is a profession directed at nurturing friendships that culminate in gifts of time, talent and treasure. There is no way that is possible without earning and maintaining trust. I love the expression that fundraising occurs at the speed of trust.

Ethics isn't an option but a necessity. We simply aren't going to be successful if donors don't have faith in us. They must have full confidence that we and the organizations we serve are going to do what we say we're going to do and fulfill their philanthropic intent.

Drafting a code of ethics for professional fundraisers was the first order of business for founders of the Association of Fundraising Professionals (AFP) in 1960. Ethics remains a top priority for AFP, serving as a guide and major asset to the more than 26,000 members in some 240 chapters who raise more than $100 billion annually. AFP has established October as Ethics Awareness Month.

Every member must sign and abide by the AFP Code of Ethical Principles and Standards. This is the strictest and only enforced code in the profession. AFP President and CEO Mike Geiger has emphasized the theme "Living Your Ethics Out Loud" and is challenging colleagues to work hard every day to ensure that ethics is integrated and elevated into all their work.

Let's step back for a moment. What do we mean by ethics?

There's a tendency to make it philosophical and abstract, but it doesn't have to be that way. Often, it can be boiled down to a simple extension of the Golden Rule.

Ethical reasoning centers on the ability to see and understand different perspectives and viewpoints, and the capacity to put yourself in someone else's shoes. It's not just knowing what's in it for you, it's weighing the impact on others.

In the fundraising profession, accountability

and transparency are touchstones for consistently doing the right thing.

Another core value is confidentiality. Fundraisers are privy to donors' personal financial information — information to which even family members sometimes don't have access. You better believe we need to keep it private.

Being good stewards of gifts is both the right and smart move. It makes it possible to go back to donors and ask that they renew and upgrade gifts.

Remuneration issues receive special attention. The AFP Standard of Professional Practice states: "Members shall not accept compensation or enter into a contract that is based on a percentage of contributions; nor shall members accept finder's fees or contingent fees."

Those involved in fundraising, both in paid and volunteer capacities, understand that gifts are seldom the result of a single relationship or moment. They reflect a dynamic process of education and engagement over time. It's unfair to reward a fundraiser for a gift that others help make possible.

Percentage compensation, commissions and finder's fees can lead to abuses and compromise the best interests of the donor. Keep in mind that several benchmarks are appropriately embraced, such as donor retention and the number of new donors acquired, the number of gifts upgraded and the number of "asks" made.

Fundraisers, when necessary, need to exercise courage. This might mean saying "no" to a gift when it comes with improper strings or standing up to our own superiors in insisting on adherence to the donor's rights.

Ethical behavior can't exist in a vacuum. It's part of a loop joining practitioners, management, boards, volunteers and donors. Together we can embrace and sustain a culture in which ethics are continually developed, encouraged and strengthened.

We all know how fiercely competitive fundraising is today. Donors receive many more requests than they can possibly fund and must choose not between the good and the bad, but between the good and the good. One ethical slip-up can wipe out the trust earned over several years with donors.

Every day I am proud to watch my colleagues throughout the non-profit community place ethics at the heart of their work, forging partnerships with donors that advance the missions of our organizations that contribute to a better world, and especially help those who are struggling.

Homework

- Does your organization have a gift acceptance policy? If not, look at the policies of comparable non-profits as a starting point.

- Do your donors — especially major gift donors — understand what they are entitled to and what they shouldn't expect?
- Discuss possible ethical dilemmas at board and staff meetings, such as major donors trying to interfere in the hiring process.
- Does your CEO, Executive Director, board chair and other senior leaders fully understand the limitations of what they can ask staff to do?
- Does your HR policy address bonuses and other incentives for reaching and surpassing performance expectations?

Now Is the Best Time

There's a popular Chinese proverb that says: "The best time to plant a tree was 20 years ago. The second-best time is now."

With major gifts by far the most efficient method of fundraising, if you don't have a program in place, though you can't go back in time, you can get started right away. How about tomorrow morning? The sooner you launch your major gifts initiative, the sooner your first or next million-dollar gift will be a reality.

Don't accept the adage that suggests your organization is too small to obtain a million-dollar gift. In fact, smaller non-profits enjoy several advantages over their larger counterparts. They can devote more attention to donor prospects. CEOs and board chairs should be personally involved in the cultivation process. And never forget that while larger non-profits can receive multiple million-dollar gifts, there is only one hero who can claim the mantle of being a non-profit's first million-dollar donor.

So, what does it take to be an effective frontline fundraiser capable of securing major gifts of $1 million and be one of a special breed that welcomes the opportunity to solicit gifts, the bigger, the better?

First all, he or she must be an incorrigible believer. They believe in the righteousness of their organizations. They believe in the better nature of donor prospects. And finally, they believe in their own abilities. Let's take a closer look at each of these beliefs.

Believing in the non-profit is like falling in love with it. Like someone you love, that doesn't mean they're perfect. But you know everything admirable and good about them, and you cherish telling their stories and answering questions about them. Your voice, face and mood unabashedly convey pride.

The best fundraisers hear "no" frequently. That's a concrete sign that they're not afraid of asking. When you overcome the fear of rejection that means you're going to hear favorable responses and facilitate a magical loop in which solicitor, donor and, especially beneficiaries, all emerge winners. After soliciting hundreds of gifts from $100 to several million dollars I'm firmly convinced that the donor derives the most satisfaction from this loop as they actualize the best of humanity in them and glow from seeing the impact of their gift dollars.

Believing in yourself as a fundraiser is not cockiness. It's a reflection of acquiring over time the knowledge and experience that replaces fear with comfort and confidence. You embrace the mechanics of the gift cycle from discovery to cultivation to solicitation to stewardship. When principles, strategies and best practices are executed consistently, they will deliver amazing results.

Second, you're not content with forging relationships. You desire friendships (as we addressed in depth in an earlier chapter) which run deep and stand the test of time. Our goal in fundraising is not a single gift transaction, but rather earning a lifetime association that steadily grows closer and closer and produces ever-increasing gifts of time and money. This is expedited by the donor prospect knowing your family and you knowing theirs.

Third, they share a relentless commitment to continuous process improvement. The most productive fundraisers are never content. You can and should learn from every solicitation, whether the response is yes, no, or maybe. Make it a habit to debrief after every solicitation and take stock of what went right and what you think you can improve on.

Fourth, effective fundraisers embody an entrepreneurial spirit for everything they do. Each donor presents a whole new set of challenges and requires flexibility in responding to their philanthropic wishes and aligning those with the mission of the non-profit. There is a steady stream of new puzzles to be solved. So, there is a fanatical desire to be creative and move the process forward.

Major gifts, particularly million-dollar gifts, usually require several meetings, or what we call "moves." We should follow up immediately — within 24 hours, if possible — on any requests expressed by the donor. This emphasizes a sense of urgency in the need for a commitment to be made sooner instead of later to bring the request and the good it will accomplish to fruition.

Finally, a ferocious commitment to the highest ethics goes hand-in-hand with a fiercely competitive spirit — as we've addressed in depth in a prior chapter. Donors must know, like, and most importantly, trust the fundraiser and their non-profit. A single ethical misstep can destroy the relationship, not to mention the friendship and the prospect of future gifts.

The successful fundraiser wants to obtain the gift, in the largest amount possible, with all their body, mind and soul. Fortunately, I've enjoyed that uplifting experience of asking for and getting major gifts to energize good works. It feels terrific. Conversely, going a long time without making an ask feels empty. It's like having your muscles atrophy because they aren't being used.

The work of frontline fundraisers is more valuable than ever. While government funding for societal benefit is being compromised, the needs that non-profits fill are escalating. Fortunately, American philanthropy is remarkably resilient. In 2023 more money was raised for non-profits than ever before — $557 billion at the phenomenal pace of approximately $1.5 billion per day or about $1 million a minute. The American people once again are demonstrating a wonderful tradition of responding, especially during tough times.

Fundraisers connect this amazing tradition of caring and sharing to a wide range of worthwhile causes that transform the world for the better. They all contribute to an improved quality of life and a brighter future.

Fundraisers aren't magicians. They are people like you and me who have trained hard to steadily improve and excel at the craft. Their lessons of success deserve emulation throughout the non-profit sector so that they can more robustly serve their beneficiaries during such a profound time of need.

Is there money out there? You bet there is. America claims about 1,000 billionaires and about 25,000,000 millionaires, and their ranks are growing every day. Plus, the numbers behind volunteerism are equally impressive. About 25% of American adults enthusiastically volunteer their time and services to bolster the missions of their favorite non-profits.

The stark reality is that non-profits could not remotely approach their impact without volunteers playing essential hands-on roles. The Independent sector estimates the value of a volunteer hour at $33.49. Volunteers are always more likely to financially support your non-profits. In other words, the traffic lights for major gifts including at the million-dollar level are definitely signaling "green."

I enjoy closing my workshops and webinars with a telling quote from the late poet Maya Angelou, who said that "people will forget what you said, people will even forget what you did, but people will never forget how you made them feel." Whether in person or virtually, your job is to make your donor prospects feel like the most important people in the world and to give them opportunities to do something special and feel great. Giving your non-profit a first million-dollar gift will certainly place them squarely in the category of doing something remarkable and make them feel like they're on top of the world.

We look forward to hearing about your million-dollar gift results!

Homework

- Do you have a major gifts program in place? If so, how is it documented?
- What are the funding priorities that will be addressed in your major gifts program?

- How do you measure the effectiveness of your major gifts initiative?
- If you don't have a program, what steps can you take immediately to initiate its organization and launch?
- Do you need outside expertise to help guide your major gifts program? If so, how will you pay for this expertise?

Acknowledgments

We are the sum of our life's experiences and especially all those who have touched us and whom we have touched during our journey. I consider myself especially fortunate that so many remarkable men and women have been part of my journey, and have provided wisdom, experience, advice and counsel that cannot be measured. Thank you for the awesome way you have lifted me up over the past 71 years.

Million-Dollar Donors

*Neil Griffin, retired bank executive, $1 million for scholarship endowment (2010), $2.5 million to add to scholarship endowment, nursing program capital improvements and unrestricted purposes (2017)

Richard Liu, Managing Director, Superior Leather Holdings, Hong Kong, $1 million for US-China exchange programs (1998)

*Dr. Janice Mendelson, retired U.S. Army colonel and surgeon, $2.2 million for Folk Life

Culture Center and unrestricted purposes
(1998)
Harvey Najim, Founder, Najim Charitable
Foundation, $1 million for scholarships (2016)
Deceased

Mentors

*Titles are listed as they were at the time of our
working relationship.*

Mike Beldon, Chairman, Alamo Colleges
Foundation, for leading with a keen
appreciation of pushing as hard as you can but
not wasting resources.

Dr. Bruce Bublitz, Dean, College of Business,
University of Texas at San Antonio, for
exemplifying a relentless openness to new
ideas and possibilities.

The Hon. Henry Cisneros, former Secretary of
U.S. Department of Housing and Urban
Development, for demonstrating that
brilliance, charisma and compassion can come
all in the same package.

John Donohue, Executive Director for
Development, University of Texas at San
Antonio, for teaching me the mechanics of
advancement.

Laura Fredricks, Founder, The Expert on the ASK,
for demonstrating that simply being
considered the best in your respective field
isn't good enough.

Dr. Jim Gaertner, Dean, College of Business, University of Texas at San Antonio, for teaching by example an in-person winning approach for asking.

The Hon. Charlie Gonzalez, U.S. House of Representatives (D-Texas) 1999 to 2013, for continuing an inspiring family commitment to public service.

Andrea Kihlstedt, Co-Founder, Capital Campaign Pro, for her presentation at an AFP conference which started me dreaming that I would like to become a fundraising trainer/consultant.

Jimmy LaRose, Co-Founder, National Association of Nonprofit Organizations & Executives, and author of *Re-Imagining Philanthropy*, for living the role of the ultimate truth teller.

Dr. Robert Lengel Associate Dean for Executive Education, College of Business, University of Texas at San Antonio, for boldly challenging us to step outside ourselves and think in new and different ways.

Marv LeRoy, President & Founder, Institute for Philanthropic Excellence, for being an amazing friend and colleague who, by his example, demonstrates the power of dreaming big.

Dr. Bruce Leslie, Chancellor, Alamo Colleges, for exemplifying an amazing ability to always remain cool under any circumstances.

Dr. Tessa Martinez Pollock, President, Our Lady of the Lake University, for demonstrating

vision, incredible communication skills and a
sense of enriching the impoverished
community surrounding the university.

*Edith McAllister, Grandest of Grande Dames, for
loving doing good works and having a good
time simultaneously.

*Red McCombs, Chairman, McCombs Enterprises,
for first suggesting that I consider a career in
development.

Allen Paul, Executive Director, Agriculture
Council of America, for putting me on the
right path for the rest of my career from a
position of zest and strength.

Barbara Radnofsky, Founder, Radnofsky
Mediation Services, for teaching that no
problem is too difficult to resolve.

Art Riklin, Owner, Arthur Riklin Insurance, for
introducing me to a wide range of business
and community leaders.

*Sam Riklin, CEO, Riklin Advertising &
Marketing, for bringing me into his office for
six months, an experience that was the
equivalent of earning an MBA.

Lionel Sosa, Advertising/PR/Marketing Pioneer,
for reminding us that regardless of how
extraordinary past accomplishments are, you
can still continue growing.

Rabbi Sam Stahl, Rabbi Emeritus, Temple
Beth-El, for guiding my spiritual journey.

Larry Vaclavik, Managing Principal, Dini Spheris,

for showing me that successful fundraisers can and should be highly ethical and highly competitive at the same time.

Anthony White, Chairman, Alamo Colleges Foundation, for always leading by capturing the wisdom of the whole.

Dr. Bob Ziegler, President, San Antonio College, for demonstrating that leaders are great listeners and learn from those who work for them.

* Deceased

Colleagues

The following practitioners have partnered with me on live workshops, webinars, podcasts and writing projects, consistently making work fun.

Mercedes Alhaj, COO, The Nonprofit Council

Marcy Andrade, Executive Director, Assistance League of San Antonio

Armen Babajanian, CEO, World Affairs Council of San Antonio

Dan Baker, President, National Peace Corps Association

Nikisha Baker, CEO, SAMMinistries

Hunter Beaton, Founder & CEO, Day1 Bags

Mike Bennett, Principal, Interim CEO Consulting

Catherine Bishop, Partner & Director Employee Benefits, Catto & Catto

Sally Bryant, CEO, BRYANT GROUP

Ellen Bristol, President, Bristol Group

Melissa Brown, Principal, Melissa S. Brown & Associates, LLC

Mike Buckley, Managing Partner/Founder, The Killoe Group

Frank W. Burns, Jr., Television Programming, City of San Antonio

Ben Case, CEO & Senior Consultant, Focused on Fundraising

Mike Davis, unofficial dean of the San Antonio fundraising community

Gloria Delgado, Community Development Specialist, Texas Capital Bank

Alex Dunn, Founder, Millionaire Grant Lady

Louis Fawcett, President, National Association of Nonprofit Organizations & Executives

Howie Feinberg, CEO, Hebrew Free Loan Association of San Antonio

Jay Frost, CEO, Frost on Fundraising

Kristen Hay, Marketing Manager, Bloomerang

Chancellor Kent Hance, Podcast Host, Best Storyteller in Texas

Marcy Heim. Founder. The Artful Asker

Rev. Wydnee Holbrook, Executive Director, Interfaith San Antonio Alliance

Marjorie Hope, Author, *CONNECTIPLOMACY*

Diana Hoyt, Chief Strategist & Trainer, Formula for Fundraising

Leia Hunt, Founder/Executive Director, Leia's Kids

Jeff Jowdy, President, Lighthouse Counsel

Shelia Klein, Former President, Assistance League of San Antonio

Cody Knowlton, President & CEO, Baptist Health
    Foundation of San Antonio
Anne Krause, Vice President of Advancement,
    Texas 2036
John Largent, CEO, Largent Media
Jon Levy, Founder & Host, Influencers
Dona Liston, Owner, Lambermont Events
Katie Lord, Vice President, Non-Profit
    Development, PROOF
Kasey Lowe, Senior Director of Development,
    Water4
Jay Love, Co-Founder, Bloomerang, and Co-
    Founder, Launch Cause
Gabe Lowe, Principal, Blk Sheep Marketing
Charlotte-Anne Lucas, Executive Director,
    NOWCast SA
Karl Miller Lugo, Vice President, Advancement &
    Alumni Engagement, University of Texas at
    San Antonio.
Rhanda Luna, Director of Corporate Giving &
    Events, SAFE
Deborah Martin, Major Gifts Officer, Alamo
    Colleges Foundation
Scott McAninch, CEO, The Nonprofit Council
Jenny Moore, Associate Clinical Professor,
    Communication & Founding Director of
    Jaguar Student Media, Texas A&M University
    -San Antonio
Kelli Newman, President, Newman & Newman,
    Inc.

Dr. Richard Ortega, former Chief Development Officer for multiple non-profits

Marc Pitman, Founder, Concord Leadership Group

Dylan Pyne, Senior Director of Development, Volunteer New York!

Larry Raff, President, Copley Raff

Dr. Mark Raizen, Founder & Chairman, The Pointsman Foundation

Bernard Ross, Director, =mc consulting

Michael Rubin, President, Michael D. Rubin & Associates

Brian Saber, President, Asking Matters

Amir Samandi, Founder & Executive Director, Students of Service

Patrick Schmitt, Co-Founder, Free Will

Ron Sellars, Founder, Gray Matter Research & Consulting, LLC

Meghan Speer, Author, *Nonprofit Hub*

Curt Slangal, Owner, Slangal South Studio

Fred Steubing, Wealth Advisory Specialist, Broadway Bank

Callum Stewart, Chief Development Officer, Georgetown University Walsh School of Foreign Service

Abbie J. von Schlegell, FAFP (one of only 10 distinguished fundraising practitioners to receive this highest distinction from Association of Fundraising Professionals)

Erica Waarsdorp, President, A Direct Solution

Jack Warkenthien, CEO & Founder, NextStep Solutions

Dr. Julie Wiernik, Owner, Texas Center for Sport Psychology

Reggie Williams, former President and CEO San Antonio Area Foundation and former Senior Vice President IT Operations, USAA

Carolyn Young, former team member at both Our Lady of the Lake University and Alamo Colleges Foundation.

Friends of a Lifetime

Amy Al-Haj, Dan Barkin, Ruth Bracken, Arturo Burgueno, Pete Baldwin, Dr. Steve Cross, Seth Greenberg, Al Hartman, Allan Smith, David Kanter, Merrill Kirshenbaum, Larry Kosow, Larry Lamb, Woody Lawson, Carolyn & Tim Lay, Dr. Jon Lubitz, Gene Marck, Chris Murray, Bartley O'Hara, Dr. Charles Pozner, John Pozner, Bob Radano, Norma Remick, Laura and Mike Richardson, and Dr. Abby Gray Stonerock.

Family

Andrea Eskin, who entered my life and made everything better; Don & Sandy Eskin, super spouse who supported his wife in leading 23 Jimmy Memorial golf tournaments raising more than $2 million to fight cancer; Barbara Eskin & Ed Barry, for teaching the power of contrarian thinking and to embrace new technologies; Abby Eskin, Zak Smith, Zoe Eskin and Smith Eskin, the next generation devoted to protecting the planet; and Mark Sheinkopf, the cousin who celebrates humor and the Boston Celtics.

In Memoriam

David Eskin, for teaching me to cherish the success of friends; Charlotte Eskin, for teaching me how to make a mockery of ageism; and Dr. Alex Kusko, for extending and enriching my mother's life.

About the Author

After nearly 30 years as a fundraising professional, Jim Eskin launched Eskin Fundraising Training, LLC, in 2018. Since then he has hosted numerous workshops, webinars, podcasts and TV interviews with renowned professionals on topics of interest to professional and volunteer non-profit leaders around the world. Workshops and board training sessions that he conducts provide the coaching and support services non-profits need to compete for and secure private gifts. He has authored hundreds of guest columns for newspapers, business journals and blogs, and publishes *Stratagems*, a free monthly e-newsletter exploring timely issues and trends in philanthropy, advocacy, and image. Jim's first book, *10 Simple Fundraising Lessons*, a common-sense guide to overcoming your fear of asking for gifts, was published in 2019 and can be purchased on Amazon in either printed or electronic format.

For detailed information about virtual individualized training for your non-profit's staff, board and volunteers, or to subscribe to Jim's free newsletter and receive information about upcoming free programs, visit www.eskinfundraisingtraining.com. You can also follow Eskin Fundraising Training on Facebook and read more of Jim's articles on fundraising by connecting with him on LinkedIn. Contact Jim by email at jeskin@aol.com.

Non-Profit North Stars

Do you know a staff or board member, volunteer or donor who deserves special recognition for their service, commitment and leadership in the non-profit sector? Eskin Fundraising Training would like to salute them on our "Non-Profit North Stars" podcast series.

Each episode focuses on an "unsung hero" who fuels the aspirations and achievements of any non-profit from around the country. Nominees may be professional staff, board members, volunteers, donors or others who propel the mission of the non-profit by their inspiring examples. Honorees will also be featured in our monthly e-newsletter Stratagems and other communications, as well as on social media.

You can listen to the podcast series online by searching for **Non-Profit North Stars with Jim Eskin**. To send in your nomination, fill out the form at: https://lp.constantcontactpages.com/sv/StcYPp2 or contact Jim directly at jeskin@aol.com for more information.